TONY GARCIA

Spread Hope Like Fire

First published by 1428 Publishing in 2018

Copyright © Tony Garcia, 2018

All rights reserved. No part of this publication may be reproduced, stored or transmitted in any form or by any means, electronic, mechanical, photocopying, recording, scanning, or otherwise without written permission from the publisher. It is illegal to copy this book, post it to a website, or distribute it by any other means without permission.

First edition

ISBN: 9781722252199

Contents

Foreword	v
Today, Day One	1
THAT SEED OF SELF DOUBT	4
WITHDRAWING	6
YOU ARE YOUR BIGGEST FAN	9
LIFE'S NOT FOR ME	12
EVERY STEP YOU TAKE	14
ONCE UPON A TIME	16
SITTING IN MY MIND	18
LOSS	20
FORGIVENESS DOES NOT = RECONCILIATION	22
IT DOESN'T MATTER	24
HOW DO YOU FEEL?	25
I KNOW I'M NOT PERFECT	26
SHOULDA WOULDA COULDA	28
WHAT ARE YOU LOOKING FOR?	30
WHY DO WE FALL?	32
Weakness or Help?	34
THE RULE OF THREE	36
CONFIDENCE	38
TUNE INTO YOURSELF	40
RISE UP	42
ABSOLUTE SOLUTION TO A TEMORARY PROBLEM	44

WHAT'S MY DESTINY?	46
THE PROCESS	48
CONECTIONS	50
LET'S PLAY THE BLAME GAME	52
YOU'RE DEFEATED BEFORE YOU EVEN GET GOING	54
DON'T LIE TO YOURSELF	56
OWN YOUR LIFE	58
THERE ARE OTHERS	60
WAKE UP	62
THE SWITCH	64
FIGHTING TO GROW	66
THE WAYSIDE	69
WHEN IT'S ALL DONE	71
PEAKS AND VALLEYS	73
YOU'RE THE REASON	75
DON'T BE AFRAID	77
AT MY LOWEST	79
AT MY HIGHEST	81
ABOUT THE AUTHOR	82

Foreword

Life, most of us live it wanting to achieve greatness, achieve tremendous moments, but is life truly made up of these moments of greatness? Oddly enough no. Life is made of simple moments. These simple moments are what define us as people. Are we happy with who we have become, or are we drowning in disappointment? Rarely, life will turn out in which we planned it, but, such is life, for many the unexpected occurs; it takes us and surprises us with new possibilities. I found this moment of sitting here writing this book to be something of a challenge. I never thought I would achieve this moment again. My life did not turn out in which the way I planned it, but here I am writing. I started out at the age of eighteen wanting to change lives through filmmaking. I tried my hand at this for many years and finally put my film tools away for good. Feeling defeated it was time to walk away from a passion I had since I was a kid. I found myself wondering what life had in store for me? I felt lost at times; I felt a little depressed at times, to be honest, I felt extremely depressed most of the time. I was not a very religious man at the time, but about five years ago I found myself at an all-time low in my life. I was stuck. So, I turned to something I had not done in a long time, I prayed. I turned to

God the creator of life, beauty, joy, love, and understanding for his guidance. The answer that finally came was, nothing. There was no awe awakening answers or thunderous voice that came from the heavens above. Looking back now I can say that I was mistaken. I did receive a thunderous answer. The journey that was laid in front of me was in fact to change the world. I met a man that I paid $120 an hour each week to be my friend. This man is my therapist. With his help, I found that I was not alone when it came to feelings of depression, sorrow, or pain. I once again found a new meaning in my life. I wanted to help others that felt the same pain as me. A hero of mine, Robin Williams once said, "I think the saddest people always try their hardest to make people happy because they know what it's like to feel absolutely worthless and they don't want anyone else to feel like that." This is my path; this is my meaning in life, I too want to follow in the footsteps of my friend/therapist and charge $120 an hour to hopefully someday have helped someone when they were lost. Know that I helped them find their way again. I thankfully obtained my bachelor's degree in psychology and am currently working on my master in marriage and family therapy. I also started the podcast of Spread Hope Like Fire to reach those that felt alone. Now I sit here writing a book in hopes to do the same and reach even more people. I write this book as a daily reminder that you are not alone, this book is an open door for those that hope to spark a fire of hope. I hope you can read each daily entry that will spark your fire, spark your hope, and now I proudly stand on my two feet looking out at new possibilities.

One

Today, Day One

I know you come here maybe at an all-time low, reading these

words and thinking how do you get out of this hole that I'm in?

Today may have been tough for you. This month may have been

rough, or maybe these past years have been a period of despair?

Things in life may not have gone the way in which you would have

liked. Life may be chipping away at you, and you have reached this point in life where you see no light. Maybe your job, relationship,

family, the financial situation has buried you in a dark abyss. Or

perhaps you are like me? You suffer from a mental disorder.

Anxiety? Depression? Pain? Suffering in silence? So how do we fix

this? The simple answer is that you were given another day. You

were given a chance to make a change. Make a difference that

starts now. It won't be easy, trust me. I've been right where you are

looking for something to spark that hope. I know it may seem

overwhelming, or impossible. Remember you were given this day

for a reason. Are you going to stay in the darkness or are you going

to take that step into the light? It may seem scary to take a step into

the unknown, but that is what that step is, unknown. Many

are

scared of the thought of not knowing or planning each and every

aspect of our life, but life will not turn out in many aspects for which

you have intended. Take that fear, turn it into fuel that lights the

flame that allows you to take that step and illuminate your life. Take

that lifeline and walk forward out into a world that is new and

exciting. Fear can hold you back, it kept me back for years, but there

is a life that can exist where you are truly happy. It is just going to

take you to make that choice of whether or not you want to reach

out and grab YOUR happiness.

Two

THAT SEED OF SELF DOUBT

I'm guilty! Most of my pitfalls and let downs have been a result of that little seed which I

planted in my own mind, that seed of self- doubt. This led to self-pity, which ultimately

led to self-destruction. Have you self-sabotaged yourself in life? I know I have. Have you

ever thought that you were not worth anything other than failure? I have. Have you ever

given up before you even try? I have. This is self-sabotaging yourself. You become what

is known as a self- fulfilling prophet. You are able to tell the

THAT SEED OF SELF DOUBT

future because you are

writing your future right now. Every choice, every thought, every step that you take is

what will define you. Make these choices that will lead you to success and lead you into a

life that is filled with joy. A simple positive thought that you send out into the world will

come back to grant you that success that is what you have yarned for. Trust that

positivity can take you far in life just as negativity has deeply buried you. You see these

two points of negative and positive outlooks have been defining you to this very

moment. Are you going to be able to say that you believed in yourself and in turn gain so

much more from being your own supporter? Make your mind work for you.

Three

WITHDRAWING

Those moments we all face when depression hits, we isolate. Those that care for us

question just what we are doing, why we don't come around, why we don't return phone
calls, why we stay locked away in our home? Withdrawing is something I do, and I used

to do often. I wouldn't want to face the world, because the world to me is a dark, scary

place. Just stepping outside of the door to have to go to work at times was a struggle but I

had to do it. The isolating of our self is a protection mechanism, but what are we

WITHDRAWING

protecting our self from? Those that love us and care for us want to help, but they just

seem not to understand what it is that we hide from, we hide from our own fears,

emotions, sadness, and hurt. But, this isolating and withdrawing is not shielding us

from these emotions, it is leaving us helpless and at the mercy of these thoughts and

emotions that attack us when we are at our weakest, when we are alone. Have you ever

stopped to think that choosing to isolate makes the situation and outside of the door to

have to go to work at times was a struggle but I had to do it. The isolating of our self is a

protection mechanism, but what are we protecting our self from? Those that love us and

care for us want to help, but they just seem not to understand what it is that we hide

from, we hide from our own fears, emotions, sadness, and hurt. But, this isolating and

withdrawing is not shielding us from these emotions, it is

leaving us helpless and at the

mercy of these thoughts and emotions that attack us when we are at our weakest, when

we are alone. Have you ever stopped to think that choosing to isolate makes the situation

and the thoughts worse? How about today you try to decide to do something you may

have never done before, reach out to those that support you whether it be a friend,

parent, family member, co- worker, or whoever is within your support system and just

talk. Trust me talking helps.

Four

YOU ARE YOUR BIGGEST FAN

Are you lying in bed reading this? I hope so because after you read this, I want you to get
up

out of bed and seize the day. You were given another shot at another day. You have this

opportunity that many don't, another day. No one is going to build you up and achieve

life's goals like yourself. No one is going to put in the work to life for you, but you. No

one is going to lift you up like you can lift yourself up! You have to become your biggest

fan, not your worst enemy. You have to cheer yourself on not boo yourself out of the

room. You have to take this day and every day and conquer it. No matter what life throws

at us, we have to kick its teeth down its throat and conquer. Too many times we are our

own worst enemies. We are too harsh on ourselves, and this is where we fall down, and

many times stay down. You have to pick yourself up and charge forward at life. We all

have today to make life worth living because we don't know if we get to do this

tomorrow, or even an hour from now. You have to become your best friend, and you have

to become your biggest fan and stop worrying about what others think. When it comes

down to it what others think NEVER MATTERS! When the day is done, and you are laying

back in your bed with your own thoughts all that matters is that you conquered the day

YOU ARE YOUR BIGGEST FAN

in what you wanted to achieve and those that doubted you would see that their opinions

are just their weaknesses that they couldn't accomplish what you have accomplished.

Five

LIFE'S NOT FOR ME

I have recently been reading about all these celebrity suicides that have occurred, and the

question that is posed is, is life not for me? Have you asked yourself this question? Has

life challenged you so harshly that you think life is not for me? Maybe your relationship

with someone has just ended, perhaps you have lost a loved one, perhaps you have lost

your job, your home, a pet, maybe your finances are not in a good spot, and perhaps you

thought life is not for me? You may think life is treating you unfairly, but you believe

this! Own your thoughts. Own your situation, own your life. You think life is treating you

unfairly, but this is when you must stay strong. Yes, this is easier said than done, but

stay strong! All these life challenges leave us many times not knowing what to do, but

you have a choice right now, CHANGE YOUR THINKING! You can take control, you may

struggle for a while, but you will get through this, and the funny thing is that life will

surprise you. There will always be new possibilities.

Six

EVERY STEP YOU TAKE

As I've said before, life rarely turns out the way in which we plan it. Refocus your

thoughts from what can go wrong to what can go right. We as humans struggle each and

every day with anxiety, and we try to plan out our day, our week, our month, our year,

our life, even our next few steps, but how often do these plans work out that way? It's

going to take some practice but take each day as it comes and stop planning every step of

every moment. Take a look around and appreciate the smaller

things in life that are

going right for you at the moment, because there are those in the world that wish they

had your life. This says a lot, that there are those in life that are struggling with greater

obstacles far worse than what you are going through right at this moment. By

appreciating the things in life that you have, no matter how small they may be, stopping

just to appreciate and be thankful for that breath of air you just took can mean so much

because there are those that are taking their last breaths. Stop planning and start
appreciating.

Seven

ONCE UPON A TIME

Once upon a time, you were here to guide me and protect me
   You taught me, love
   You taught me strength

   You taught me life
   Once upon a time, we lived in a castle built upon what are now treasured memories
   My hands you would hold
   My fears you would banish
   My pain you would heal Once upon a time, I was your baby Time passed on, and I held

   your hand
   Your fears I battled

   Your pain I wish I could take for you
   Once upon a time lived a mother I called her mom

ONCE UPON A TIME

You were lucky to have met her But she has now gone

She lives on forever
She is gone but not far

One day we will meet again

Until then you can live in my heart Once upon a time

I still miss you, mom,

I wrote this poem while sitting in the waiting room of UCLA medical center one

afternoon while my mom was getting a test done to see if she had cancer. The thoughts

and emotions that I felt that moment live within me and the way in which I express this

day is through this poem. Make every effort to let your mom know just how much you

love her.

Eight

SITTING IN MY MIND

Anxiety. That little emotion that I love so much. Anxiety has robbed me of so many great

moments in my life. I can remember going to Disney World with my girlfriend and mom

one year for Christmas, and this is where people say "magic" lives. Not in my mind. In

my mind, all I thought about was what if this experience never happens again? What if

these two people I love so profoundly are not here with me tomorrow? My anxiety loves to bury everyone. I love, and I let my anxiety achieve it. I allowed it to ravish my life for

years. Maybe you can relate? Anxiety is the little devil in my head that will not stop until

I am in tears. It will not stop until I can't breathe. It won't stop until I stop living. I

stopped livening my life for many years as I found myself scared to enjoy anything other

than sitting in my mind. The shade was just the right type of darkness that I needed

while I wallowed away thinking of the worst in my mind.

STOP IT!

Stop letting these thoughts of anxiety slow you down. What has worrying every gotten

anyone?

Nine

LOSS

Today you may be struggling with the loss of a loved one. With today's technology, we

are so connected, yet so distant from one another. Sometimes we take a text message, a

phone call, a social media reply for granted. For myself, I have always looked at greeting

cards that people have given me over the years. I have saved every single card that I

was ever given whether it be for birthdays, congratulations, or sorry for your loss, I save every card. I know that life is rushed we all have tasks to get done today and every day

and that slowing down is something that is hard to do but don't take these people in

your life for granted, because one day they won't be there. Those phone calls on your call

log, those text messages received that you never replied to, those birthday cards, those

social media interactions, and definitely those facebook memories we all get notified of

every day will be all that we have left of that person. Their memory. So, make today

count with those that you love. Text them, call them, facebook them, twitter them, reach

out and make the love you have count while there is still time. It's not how you

remember the person that has passed away and the lovely things people say to keep their

memory alive, but what counts is how you treat them while they are here still on this

earth with you.

Ten

FORGIVENESS DOES NOT = RECONCILIATION

As you may know, if you listen to the podcast that I had a pretty lousy childhood with my

Dad. He mentally and verbally abused me. This got me to start thinking how about how

many people around me view forgiveness and how they will share their (many times

unsolicited) thoughts about the subject. I learned that forgiveness is for me not for my

father. Forgiveness is allowing me to move on with my life and move forward with a new

FORGIVENESS DOES NOT = RECONCILIATION

and clean slate, but for many, I've always been told that "if you truly forgive someone

that means you wipe the slate clean with them and you allow them to rebuild a

relationship with you", BUT FORGIVENESS IS NOT RECONCILIATION

Trust me I checked the dictionary.

Eleven

IT DOESN'T MATTER

It doesn't matter how much money you have. It doesn't matter how many friends you

have. It doesn't matter how you look. It doesn't matter how bad your relationships are

because every single new day that you are given is a chance to erase your past struggles,

hurts, wants, failures, and pain, and today you have the opportunity to write a new

future.

Twelve

HOW DO YOU FEEL?

Our life is based on the way we feel. Use today to attract what you want in your life. The

biggest problem that we face is our feelings. If we wake up on the wrong side of the bed

today and go out into the world with these feelings of negativity the world will gravitate

that negativity right into your life. Yes, there will be obstacles in life that come our way,

but the majority of our life is 100% based on the way in which we feel. So, how do you

feel?

Thirteen

I KNOW I'M NOT PERFECT

I know I've made mistakes.
  I know I'm not the richest.

  I know I've hurt others.

  I know I'm not the smartest.

  I know I'm not the prettiest.

  I know I'm not always going to succeed.

  BUT

  I'm perfectly imperfect, and I'm going to take today to make it count.

  I'm going to take that step forward with pride.

I KNOW I'M NOT PERFECT

I'm going to reach out to that one person I've neglected.

I'm going to give encouragement to those that need it.

I'm going to live my life today.

I know I may not get another chance.

I know that tomorrow may never come.

I know I must do all that I can for this moment.

Fourteen

SHOULDA WOULDA COULDA

You were born for a reason. You were placed here on earth to accomplish so much, but do

you let yourself get held back? Do you allow what others think to keep you from your

goals and dreams? Don't allow someone ever to hold you back. Too many times we make

excuses for why or how we did not achieve our goals, and in many cases, it's because we

are scared of what others think. Don't ever let someone tell you that you are not good

enough, never let someone talk you out of your dreams, don't ever give up. People that

talk you down from achieving are misleading. They as well are too scared to achieve, so

they deceive others. The more you listen, the more miserable you'll become. Life is a

graveyard of broken dreams. If you never follow your dreams, you'll one day find

yourself looking back on your life thinking about what could have been? So do you live

for others or do you live for yourself?

Fifteen

WHAT ARE YOU LOOKING FOR?

Recently I had gone through a situation that I thought I would not survive. We usually

find what we're looking for in life. For me, I spent a good chunk of my life in a battle with

my anxiety and thinking something horrific was going to happen. Something tragic

would occur. I spent so much time in the future that I lost my gifts in the present.

Everyone would ask why I thought this way? I had no idea, to be honest. My anxiety took

over my life so significantly that I finally found what I had

WHAT ARE YOU LOOKING FOR?

been looking for. I was given

news that ended a relationship. The woman I loved so greatly had finally reached her

breaking point, and I was left standing with what I had sought out so much. Heartache

and pain. My anxiety had took control and would always whisper to me that I was

undeserving, I was worthless, and that she was going to leave me. My anxiety was

tearing my girlfriend and I apart and I let it, as that is what I was looking for, that was

what I was predicting, I allowed myself to believe the anxiety and now I ask, what is it

that you are looking for?

Sixteen

WHY DO WE FALL?

Why do we fall? I always think of Alfred from the *Dark Knight* when I ask myself this

question. If you have seen the movie, you know the answer, but sometimes it's not as

easy to get back up. You find it hard to get back up when you have been put down so

many times, you find it hard to get back up especially when you have tried numerous

times but just can't stand up on your own two feet. But what if that person that that

keeps putting you down is yourself? The fears that we have

are something that

sometimes cripples us. The fear of being in financial despair, the fear of failure, the fear

of not succeeding, the fear of not having enough, the fear of not being loved, the fear of

being alone, the fear of never obtaining financial freedom, the fear of self-doubt, the

doubt that you believe you are not worthy of achieving the success you want out of life.

How do you get back up? We have the ability to adapt, react, reevaluate. What is truly

important in your life? What do you have that others would be so content and grateful to

have? Life is made up of small moments that we all take for granted and we all need to

appreciate what we have in order to get back up, to stand proud, to look at those

accomplishments that you do have and to appreciate the air you are breathing.

Appreciate the small things in life to build up your strength in order to get back up.

Seventeen

Weakness or Help?

Have you ever come across a person angry, grumpy, someone that lashes out at others?

Might you live with them? Maybe you're married to them? Perhaps you work with them?
What are your thoughts of these people? I used to always think of it as a sign of weakness

in the person. A weakness because they did not have the strength to control their

emotions, so they lash out. This is the farthest from the truth. When someone lashes out,

it is not a sign of weakness like we all think. It's a sign of someone crying out for help.

Weakness or Help?

Remember that next time you cross paths with that person, they are hurting, they need

help, they need comfort.

Eighteen

THE RULE OF THREE

We are all guilty of doing it. That dirty little deed. Gossiping! C'mon what did you think I

was going to say? Get your mind right my friend. I'm a huge fan of philosophy if you

haven't been able to tell, Socrates, to be exact. The power of our words is so strong that

we hardly ever think about the power they truly have. What do our words exactly do to

others? Take a second to think of a time you were on the other end of the gossiping loop

that came out of another person's mouth. Now put that into

THE RULE OF THREE

perspective in your life.

When we speak about issues, especially with dealing with others we need to take into

account three small things before we use our tongue to damage or harm others; is it

true? If you're not sure it's true, why are you willing to speak about it? Is it good news?

Why share the good news? We like talking about the negative dirt of someone else it

seems to be human nature. Lastly is it useful? Can I use this information in a good way?

Remember that we attract what we put out into the world and if we are willing to

tear someone down be sure to know that the circle of gossip will come back around, but

what will it cost you when it is your turn? So remember is it true? Is it good news? Is it

useful?

Nineteen

CONFIDENCE

One of the most significant tools that anyone can carry around in their personal tool bag

    is that of confidence. Confidence is a tool that will decide whether or not you are going to

    be successful in life. Having confidence in one's self not only is a mindset it is being

    confident in your happiness, being confident in your choices, being confident in your

    spiritual outlook, being confident in that you will make it no matter what life throws at

    you. Sadly, if you can't find confidence in yourself, you better

CONFIDENCE

believe that no one else

will find confidence in you either. Being confident is sending out into the world that

people can trust in you, people can believe in you, people can count on you, and people

can support you in all and everything you strive to achieve. Confidence is the key that we

all keep losing. So, my advice is to stop looking for the key to the door of confidence and

just kick that bad boy in.

Twenty

TUNE INTO YOURSELF

Many times, we get lost in the shuffle. I have been telling you this past month that you

need to stay connected, but now I'm going to tell you that while all of life's trails are

going on tune into yourself. Take some time for some self-care. I once had a friend that

was so busy trying to please everyone, stay in contact with everyone, stayed trying to

make everyone else happy that he forgot to make sure he was happy. He forgot that we

all need time to ourselves. We all need time to take care and evaluate where we are in life,

where we want to be headed, and accept that where we are headed may not be where we

end up. My most important message throughout this month has been to sit back and

enjoy the journey because once we reach that destination, we have no other place to go.

Make sure we take the time that we need to make sure we are happy, that we are cared

for, that our most prominent supporter is staying healthy, happy, and ready for the

journey.

Twenty-One

RISE UP

Today is a new day, it will be filled with so many events large and small, and you need to

know that you are given this day to rise up, rise up and conquer. You have this inner

strength that beckons you to the occasion. You are a warrior. When you believe in

yourself, you believe that anything is possible. When you believe in yourself, you believe

that no one or no one thing can destroy you. When you believe in yourself you believe

that you will get to the end of the day, and when you get to

RISE UP

the end of the day you may be

bruised, battered, injured, but you made it. You fought like a Trojan warrior, and you

survived. Many in this world have problems that they can't overcome, and they can't see

past these problems whether big or small. These problems take them down and take

them out of the game of life. Sadly, these people take their own life and with that, end

the battle and end the pain and suffering they just can't get over. I'm not saying they are

weak, but they battled to the end. Please fight and never give up. Rise up believe in

yourself.

Twenty-Two

ABSOLUTE SOLUTION TO A TEMORARY PROBLEM

~~~

We hear about it. We see it on television. We read about it on social media. We see those

hateful comments such as that person was so weak and didn't deserve their life. Suicide

is something that as a society is not talked about enough. Those that commit suicide are

silent about it, they will most likely never let anyone know what they are planning, they

are hurting, they are in such great pain that they will do anything to get rid of the pain,

ABSOLUTE SOLUTION TO A TEMORARY PROBLEM

but the problem is temporary, we all have to work through these problems. It may hurt,

it may be so hurtful and so hard to deal with but taking an absolute solution to a

temporary problem is not the answer. There is so much more to live for, so much that

can change, so much so that you were given another day, anther chance. Being given

another day is being given another shot at overcoming the pain and when the time does

come to where that pain is gone the opportunity will present itself to show you just how

much stronger you as a person genuinely are. Don't stay silent, share your thoughts with

someone that can help. Just because you are hurting doesn't make you weak remember

that you are loved.

Twenty-Three

WHAT'S MY DESTINY?

For many of us, we think of this question quite frequently. Why were we put on this

earth? I have nothing special to offer. I work a 9- 5 job that I hate. I have a car the barely

starts. My bank account is almost non-existent. No one really cares about me. The truth

is that God has given each and every one of us a special gift to share with the world. Mine

is to try and help others because I know that pain and suffering that many deal

with when it comes to anxiety and depression. It took me

many years to come to terms

with this gift as I always wanted to leave my mark on the earth in some way or another. I

thought for years that I was going to make movies and that I was going to impact the

world through my visions of storytelling through film, but life directed me into where I

needed to be, and that is right here writing this book, hosting the podcast, working

towards my degree to become a licensed psychologist. We all think that we are not

unique, but it may take some searching to find what is right in front of your face.

Twenty-Four

THE PROCESS

By now you must have realized that you are going to be on this road of life for quite a

long time. As we get older we become wiser, we learn from the previous year, but we also

think what and why did I do certain things in life that you feel is wrong? What could you

have changed? Why did we let our self-down? We seem to always get stuck on the

negativity of our past choices instead of focusing on the accomplishments that we

have achieved. We have trained our minds so much to stay

THE PROCESS

stuck in the negative parts

that we need to explore the positive and recognize that we have accomplished great

things. It's time to live life by leaving a positive impact, led by examples, share your

experience with those around you, love harder, and be the best you can be instead of

beating yourself up.

Twenty-Five

CONECTIONS

Have you ever let a relationship flounder? Someone text messages you, and you ignore

them because you don't view them as a priority? You send them to voicemail when they

call? These people we love but are just consumed by the world around us and consumed

with our own goals and problems that we can't see those that are around us. Maybe they

are reaching out in hopes to seek help or support with their problems that they are

drowning in. Luckily today is a new day, and there is a lifeline right in front of you. Today

is a new day to where you can make a change and rebuild relationships and rebuild the

connection that has been disconnected for a period of time. As long as there is a new day

given to us we are able to improve still, still build, still mend, still laugh, and still love

those in our lives that we may have been neglecting.

Twenty-Six

LET'S PLAY THE BLAME GAME

How often do you take a mistake that occurred in your life and blame something or

someone else for what went wrong? For me, as I mentioned I wanted to become a movie

director and had a raw experience with the industry, and I spent many years bitterly

blaming others for what occurred, but it wasn't until I took that experience and viewed it

in a different light. I took responsibility for the problem which led me to quit trying my

hand in Hollywood. I finally said it was my fault in that I did

LETS PLAY THE BLAME GAME

not do everything I should

have done to make that dream come true. It wasn't until I started taking responsibility

for my mistakes that I was finally set free from my guilt and depression by accepting my

responsibility.

Twenty-Seven

YOU'RE DEFEATED BEFORE YOU EVEN GET GOING

Good morning. Today is a new opportunity. Today holds so much potential. Are you

ready to take on the day? If your mind isn't in the right place and ready to conquer you

have been defeated before the day even begins. Staying within that positive mind frame

and knowing that you are being given a gift of a new day and know that some did not

receive this gift is a beautiful thing to know that God is with you and has given you so

YOU'RE DEFEATED BEFORE YOU EVEN GET GOING

much with just this day. Let's focus on the positive, let's keep our minds on the

opportunities that await and let's take on the day and not let the day take on us.

Twenty-Eight

DON'T LIE TO YOURSELF

Are you giving it your all? For years I would lie to everyone saying that I was working

hard towards a dream I had, but I was not giving it my all. I lied about what I planned to

accomplish, I lied about the setbacks that were holding me back from things I was not

achieving so that others would not look down on me, I lied about where I saw myself ten

years down the road, but most of all I lied to myself. I told myself malicious lies. I said to

myself that one-day success would come knocking at my

DON'T LIE TO YOURSELF

door. I lied to myself that my

   dreams would come true, but I didn't need to work so hard on them. I lied to myself so

   much I started believing the things I would tell myself. Lying to yourself sets you up to

   fail. You end up like me believing all these lies and end up left with a life unfulfilled and a

   life in left in despair.

Twenty-Nine

OWN YOUR LIFE

Many of us are not owning up to the problems that we have in our lives, and that leads us

down a slippery slope where our problems begin to own us. We become too scared to face

these problems that are in our lives, and it leaves us becoming consumed with problem

after problem, and eventually, we just run away from our problems. Like I said about

lying to ourselves we make excuses for the condition that we find ourselves in and make

excuses for why we don't have what we want out of our lives.

OWN YOUR LIFE

We see ourselves still

playing that blame game of we don't have what we want out of life because we blame our

past, past hurts, past relationships, past failures, past arguments with family, the past

things people have said about you, the past experiences that have made you a victim of

your life. It's time to own our lives and stop letting life happen to us and let us own our

life.

Thirty

THERE ARE OTHERS

Only my problems matter.
  Only my circumstances matter. Only my pains matter,
Only my heartaches matter.
  Only you would understand if you were in my shoes.
Only you would care if it happened to you.

We get into this mindset that only we have problems and our problems are the hardest to

  deal with. We get into a mindset that no one understands our challenges. We get into a

  mindset that no one else cares what we are going through but stop and realize that you

  are not alone. There are so many others that are dealing with

THERE ARE OTHERS

problems and doing so in

silence. Try reaching out to help others and see what it can do to help you solve your own

issues and problems.

Thirty-One

WAKE UP

Today someone did not get to wake up and be with their loved ones. This is a powerful

thought. Luckily you were given this day, Wake up be thankful for the family you have.

Wake up be thankful for the job that you have. Wake up be thankful for the health that

you have. Wake up be thankful for the love that you share. Wake up be thankful for the

air that you breathe.

Wake up be thankful for…….

WAKE UP

Now take a moment and think about all that you should be thankful for. It is a beautiful

day that you get to live. Take this blessing and share it with others.

Thirty-Two

THE SWITCH

With life, we have many ups and downs. Somedays we feel like we are on top of the world

then suddenly it's as if something switched on us. It may feel like you are not on track

with your life goals and aspirations, and when this occurs we as humans get tired, we get

discouraged, we get to a point that we may even want to quit. But, life, life is taking us all

to the cleaners, and we all experience these setbacks and emotions that are associated

with the setbacks. Sometimes we are so entrenched in our

own needs and wants that we

are blinded by others needs and wants. We have to put the needs of others in front of us.

In order to get that love and support, you give that love and support first. Some of us

don't look at it this way and want to receive the love first but never give out the love that

others need. We need to focus more on giving in life rather than taking in life, and in

giving in life, we will be given a life of tremendous love, support, and happiness.

Thirty-Three

FIGHTING TO GROW

You may be struggling today. You may not want to get out of bed. You may not want to

talk to anyone. You may be in a dark spot in life. Things aren't panning out, and you feel

lost and confused. We are given things in life that we do not genuinely want or

understand. As the saying goes, "hindsight is twenty, twenty." I look back at trials and

struggles that I went through. Recently my mom's general Doctor had told her that she

suspected leukemia. I remember getting the call from the

doctor explaining to me what

she thought and what was going to happen from that point on. Further testing, further

research to see if my mom indeed had leukemia. Prior to this, I had been in a full-on

bout with my anxiety and depression for the past two months. I prayed for help, but I

never felt I got any answers. Everyone would tell me to stop worrying, and that things in

my life were so good, but I didn't see this. I was fighting the words that others gave me

to help. I fought the answers God was giving me, and I didn't want to fight to grow, until

I was told my mom might have leukemia. At that moment I was given the water that was

going to allow me to grow spiritually, mentally, and emotionally. All my worrying about

things that were out of my hands got me nowhere. I had to grow and accept the things I

could not change. This was my battle to evolve. Yours might be a little different but look at all the circumstances and see what is your water that you need to grow and get

stronger at life.

Thirty-Four

THE WAYSIDE

Every day we seem to keep avoiding our problems. They fall to the wayside and that is

where they stay. These problems continue to collect and pile up while you continue to

shove them there. Eventually, you are going to end up with an enormous pile that can't

sustain any more garbage because these problems start to spill over into other aspects

of your life. One problem such as relationship issues with your partner can spillover into

you having issues with others because of all this built up

garbage that has been tossed to

the wayside. This can lead you to anger issues, emotional issues, health issues you see

where I'm going with this. As long as we keep brushing away our problems and tossing

them into the wayside we a creating a landfill that we call our life. Stop throwing aside

problems no matter how small or how large because they accumulate, and it can ravage

one's life.

Thirty-Five

WHEN IT'S ALL DONE

You know at the end of the day we all struggle with a variety of issues. Some harsher

than others, some more manageable than others, some that end relationships, but this is

our journey. When we come to the end of our journey how do we want to have written it?

For myself, I know that all I'll have are my memories (unless I get dementia, and this

was all for nothing) and I want to be able to know that I left a mark on the world. Sort of

like a ripple effect when you drop a stone in a pond. I like to think of those rippling rings

as my lifeforce going out into the world and influencing others with my actions that I

made in my life. People remembering you is a ripple, talking to someone and offering

them kind words when you see them is a ripple, there are so many small things in life

that we can do that can leave so many rippling rings in the waters of life that I strive to

make every little attempt to leave my lifeforce behind when I'm gone.

Thirty-Six

PEAKS AND VALLEYS

Growing up I had it pretty rough. We were at one-point homeless living in a car, a hotel,

or with other family members. This is no easy situation for a child to deal with and I still

deal with this anxiety as an adult. One thing that kept and continues to keep me going on

with life is the words of my mom, and she would always tell me that "we live in peaks

and valleys." At the moment we were in the valley, and it was not pretty whatsoever. One

time a kid at school found out that I was living in a motel and decided to tell the entire

school about it, the valley got darker for me then, but we didn't stay there for long as

things turned around, my mom got on her feet and we were able to rent an apartment

and there we were chugging along to the top of the peak. I know it is an uphill battle to

get to the top, but we did it, and I'm still doing it. I can remember that I learned to

appreciate the small things in life, always. Just having a roof over our head was

something that I thank God for every day of my life. As a kid, we struggled even though

we had a place to stay we had no furniture, beds, tv, or a dinner table, but as long as we

as a family had the love that is all we needed. Life will always be peaks and valleys but

make sure to appreciate the small things.

Thirty-Seven

YOU'RE THE REASON

Throughout this book I've tried to convey many things to be thankful for such as the air

we breathe, the life we live, the family we love, the job we have, but I had forgotten to

mention one crucial thing that we need to be thankful for…Our self! Some of us may

question how and why should we be grateful for our self? Why? Because there are many

people that appreciate you, love you, need you, the world would be different without

you, people would be devastated without you. You make an

immense difference in just

being you. There are so many people that care for you that need you and many times we

overlook just this simple fact that we are living, that we are thriving, that we are making

impacts, many of these impacts we truly do not know as others many times will shy

away from letting you know just how much of an impact you have made to their life. I sit

and think just how much I matter to so many people that without me many would be

lost, scared, hurt, or possibly devastated to the point that life changes them and they

never regain that person they once were. You matter to someone and that someone

matters to you. Be thankful for yourself because there is not another one of you and

there never will be.

Thirty-Eight

DON'T BE AFRAID

Many of us struggle each day with emotions and problems that it seems like we can't

find our way out of them. This reminds me of being in school and always felt too dumb to

ask a question. I never raised my hand, and I never understood what was being taught.

Be the student that asks for help. There are so many outlets that you can seek the help

that you need. As I said in my forward there was a man I paid $120 to be my friend and

this man changed my life. Now I sit here writing this book. I sit here hosting a podcast. I

sit here with a bachelors degree. I sit here stressing over finals as I'm in the middle of my

Graduate program to become a therapist. My life changed by asking for help and I urge

you to change your life and don't be afraid. Ask for help.

Thirty-Nine

AT MY LOWEST

As I said in the forward of this book that I was not a very religious man, in fact at one

point I was an atheist. I just felt that there had to be no God because I suffered so greatly,

I endured such pain, I lost so much, and there was no God there speaking to me, helping

me, showing me a way out of my pain, but I was mistaken as I was looking in all the

wrong places. In fact, I give him great gratitude for helping me with discovering my

podcast *Spread hope like fire* and being able to pour my heart into this book. I'm not

saying that if you do not find comfort within God you are going to be lost, but whatever

your higher power may be it can be just as comforting as God is to me. He helps me every

day in being able to appreciate life and spread hope like fire when I was at my lowest. I

live in peaks and valleys, but I'm climbing those peaks every day. As my dear friend Fabi

put it "We do not belong to ourselves, we belong to God and when it is our time to return

to him we must go." It's a beautiful thing to know God loves me so much and that I have

Him here at all times.

Forty

AT MY HIGHEST

Today is a new day, and today holds magic within it. I never thought I would write

another book, I never thought I would accomplish all that I have, and I want for you just

to sit back and think about all that you have in your life all that you have read from this

book, and all that you have taken from this book. I hope I was able to help in some

fashion or another. I end this book with this:

"Believe in yourselves. Dream. Try. Do good."
— Mr. George Feeny

ABOUT THE AUTHOR

Tony Garcia is an author, podcaster, and a member of the boy band Menudo
TUNE INTO THE PODCAST SPREAD HOPE LIKE FIRE!
Available
   Itune
   Soundcloud
   Google Play
   &
   All other major podcast outlets.

Also support the podcast by heading over to patreon.com/spreadhopelikefire